From Big Data to Smart Data

Advances in Information Systems Set

coordinated by
Camille Rosenthal-Sabroux

Volume 1

From Big Data to Smart Data

Fernando Iafrate

WILEY

First published 2015 in Great Britain and the United States by ISTE Ltd and John Wiley & Sons, Inc.

ISTE Ltd
27-37 St George's Road
London SW19 4EU
UK

www.iste.co.uk

John Wiley & Sons, Inc.
111 River Street
Hoboken, NJ 07030
USA

www.wiley.com

Library of Congress Control Number: 2015930755

British Library Cataloguing-in-Publication Data
A CIP record for this book is available from the British Library
ISBN 978-1-84821-755-3

Contents

Preface

This book offers a journey through the new informational "space–time" that is revolutionizing the way we look at information through the study of Big and Smart Data for a zero-latency-connected world, in which the ability to act or react (in a pertinent and permanent way), regardless of the spatiotemporal context of our digitized and connected universe, becomes key.

Data (elementary particles of information) are constantly in motion (the Internet never sleeps), and once it is filtered, sorted, organized, analyzed, presented, etc., it feeds a *continuous cycle of decision-making and actions*. Crucial for this are the relationships between the data (their characteristics, format, temporality, etc.) and their value (ability to analyze and integrate it into an operational cycle of decision-making and actions), whether it is monitored by a "human" or an "automated" process (via software agents and other recommendation engines).

The world is in motion, and it will continue to move at an increasingly faster pace. Businesses must keep up with this movement and not fall behind (their competitiveness depends on it): the key to doing so is understanding and becoming an expert on the economic environment, which since the advent of the internet has become global.

Big Data was created relatively recently (less than five years ago) and is currently establishing itself in the same way Business Intelligence (technical and human methods for managing internal and external business data to improve competiveness, monitoring, etc.) established itself at the beginning of the new millennium. The huge appetite for Big Data (which is, in fact, an evolution of Business Intelligence and cannot be dissociated from it) is due to the fact that businesses, by implementing Business Intelligence solutions and organizations, have become very skilled at using and valuing their data, whether it is for strategic or operational ends. The advent of "cloud computing" (capacity enabling technological problems to be resolved by a third party) enables businesses (small- and medium-sized businesses now also have access to these tools, whereas they were previously the reserve of the large companies that could afford them) to facilitate and accelerate the implementation of Big Data. Following its rapid expansion in the early 2000s, Business Intelligence has been looking to reinvent itself; Big Data is establishing itself in this world as an important vector for growth. With the exponential "digitization" (via the Internet) of our world, the volume of available data is going through the roof (navigation data, behavioral data, customer preferences, etc.). For those who know how to use it, this data represents value and is a real advantage for getting one step ahead of the competition.

This move forward promises zero latency and connected businesses where each "event" (collected by data) can be tracked, analyzed and published to monitor and optimize businesses processes (for strategic or operational ends). This occurs when the two worlds managing the data meet: the transactional world (that aims to automate operational business processes) and the decision-making world (a medium for monitoring and optimizing business processes). For a long time, these two worlds were separated by the barriers of data "temporality" and "granularity". The transactional world has a temporality of a millisecond, or even less for data processing that supports operational business processes, whereas the decision-making world has a temporality of several hours and in some cases even days due to the volumes, diverse and varied sources, and consolidation and aggregation necessities, etc., of data. It will be seen that using all (operational and decision-making) data is required to support decision-making processes.

Unifying the decision-making world and the transactional world will require businesses to rethink their information system so as to increase its *interoperability* (capacity to integrate with other systems) and to improve the *temporality* of the management of the data flows it exchanges. This is known as an event-driven architecture (EDA), and it enables normalized and no latency data to be exchanged between its components. The information system's use value can therefore be improved.

Fernando Iafrate
February 2015

List of Figures and Tables

LIST OF FIGURES

LIST OF TABLES

Introduction

I.1. Objectives

1) To respond to the following questions:

– What is Big Data?

– Why "Big" and why "Big" now?

– What is Smart Data?

– What is the relationship between them?

2) To compare the relationship between Big Data and its value for business (Smart Data) in a connected world where information technologies are perpetually evolving: several billion people connect to the internet and exchange information in a constant flow every day; objects will be connected to software agents in increasing numbers and we will delegate many supervision tasks to them, etc., thereby causing the number of data flows that need to be processed to rise exponentially, while also creating opportunities for people who understand how the data works. Information technologies will become a medium for new services such as domotics (managing your home online),

medical telediagnosis (using online analysis tools), or personalized marketing (sending the right message to the right customer in the right context in real-time) and many others.

3) To use a didactic, progressive approach that provides concrete examples. Driven by a strong desire to demystify the subject, we will discuss the concepts supporting this move forward and will avoid the use of extremely technical language (though it is impossible to avoid completely).

4) To understand why the applications of Big Data and Smart Data are a reality, and not merely a new "buzz word" passed on from players in the computer industry (and more specifically in Business Intelligence).

5) To answer the majority of the questions you might have about Big Data and, more importantly, to spark your interest and curiosity in the domain of Business Intelligence (that encompasses Big Data). The boundaries of the domain are not always easy to define as each new realization, reflection, etc., shifts its borders. Big Data is no exception. Big Data involves great creativity, in terms of both the architecture supporting the system and its implementation within business processes.

I.2. Observation

The majority of businesses use the information (often generated by their own information system, via their transactional solutions whose aim is to improve the productivity of operational processes) they have in one way or another to monitor and optimize their activities. Businesses have had to implement decision support tools (Business Intelligence or Decision Support Systems) and appropriate organizations for processing and distributing the information throughout the Enterprise. The most mature businesses in terms of Business Intelligence have put in place Business Intelligence Competency Centers (BICCs), cross-functional organizational structures that combine Information Technology (IT), business experts and data analysts to manage the company's Business Intelligence needs and solutions. Since the dawn of time, *"mankind has wanted to know to be able to act"*, and it has to be said that businesses which have an excellent understanding of their data, decision tools, and have a Business Intelligence organization in place, have a real advantage over their competitors (better anticipation, better market positioning, better decision-making processes, higher productivity and more rational actions that are based on facts, rather than on intuition).

For a number of years, this observation has fed an entire sector of the computer industry connected to Business Intelligence, historically known as Decision Support Systems. Its aim is to provide decision support tools (it is no longer considered possible that an operational process or system has no monitoring solution) to different strategic or operational decision makers. This model has been "jeered at" from far and wide by the fast paced "digitalization" of our world (the volume of available data keeps increasing, but we still need to be able to process and take value from it). This "digitalization" linked to the internet, has prompted significant changes in consumer behavior (more information, more choice, faster, wherever the consumer might be, etc.), thus making monitoring, follow-up and optimization increasingly complicated for businesses.

Web 2.0 (or Internet 2.0) has moved in the same way. For a long time, the Internet (Web 1.0) was the "media" and internet users were "passive" to online information. There were little or no opportunities for internet users to produce information online; web content was essentially "controlled" by professionals. From the beginning of Web 2.0, we can, however, start to speak of the "democratization" of the web with the advent of blogs, social networks, diverse and varied forums, etc.: internet users practically became the "media" (more than half of online content is now generated by internet users themselves). A direct consequence of this is that the relationship between the producer (businesses) and the consumers (clients) has changed. Businesses now have to get used to what other channels are saying about them (blogs, forums, social networks, etc., fed by their clients), beyond their own external communication channels (run by the business). Businesses wanting to follow and anticipate their clients' expectations therefore have to "collaborate" with them. This more collaborative model is taken from a new branch of Business Intelligence, known as Social Media Intelligence. This branch enables businesses to listen, learn and then act on social networks, forums, etc. prompting a more "social" (and more transparent) approach to the relationship between businesses and their customers. Businesses must increasingly rely on representatives (ambassadors) to promote their image, products, etc., on this type of media. The volume and variety (blogs, images, etc.) of the data available continues to grow (the web is full of words), which via capillarity generates a saturation (or even an inability to process) of the Business Intelligence solutions in place. "Too much data kills data" and, in the end, the business risks losing value. This brings us back to Smart Data, which gives businesses, the ability to be able to identify data following these two main approaches:

1) The "interesting" data approach is data that is of interest, though not immediately so. It feeds decision-making

and action processes and will help to build the business' information heritage. This approach is more exploratory; less structured and enables analysts to discover new opportunities which may become "relevant" at a later date.

2) The "relevant" data approach is data from which actions can be conceived. It will feed decision-making and action processes. Relevant data is at the heart of "Smart Data".

In this digitalized, globalized and perpetually moving world, in which mobility (ability to communicate using any type of device in any location) associated with temporality (any time) has become key, being able to communicate, act and react in almost real-time is no longer a desire for businesses, but rather an obligation (the internet never sleeps as it is always daytime somewhere in the world). "My Time", "My Space", "My Device" is now a natural expectation from the users

We will now outline the history of Business Intelligence.

I.2.1. *Before 2000 (largely speaking, before e-commerce)*

At this time, we talked about Decision Support Systems rather than Business Intelligence (a term that was hardly used at all). The domain was seen as extremely technical and mostly used Executive Information Systems (EISs). Data was managed in a very "IT-centric" way.

The main problem was the Extract, Transform, Load (ETL) process, that is, extracting, storing and analyzing data from a business' transactional system to reproduce it to different users (small numbers connected to the business' very centralized management model) via decision-making platforms (production of dashboards). "Data cleansing" (controlling the integrity, the quality, etc. of data often from heterogeneous sources) became the order of the day, which posited the principle that bad data causes bad decisions. Not all of these processes were automated (although the evolution of ETLs enabled processing chains to be better integrated) and were often very long (updating consolidated data could take several days). Therefore, the IT department was a very "powerful" player in this (very technical) move. The decision-making structure (that included solutions as well as the production of reports, dashboards, etc.) was very "IT-centric" and was an obligatory step for the implementation of solutions, as well as the management of data and reports for the business departments (the "consumers" of this information). In a short space of time, the model's inefficiencies came to the fore: it had restrictions (often connected to IT resources) that limited its ability to respond to businesses' growing requirements for "reporting". "Time to Market" (the time between demand and its implementation) became a real problem. The response to the issue was organizational: business information competency centers were implemented to deal with the management and publication of information throughout the business, representing the first step toward BICCs.

Access to decision-making systems was not very widespread (not just for technical reasons, but also because businesses chose it to be so) as decision-making centers were centralized to the general management (later, the globalization of the business shacked this model, and enterprises reacted by implementing distributed and localized decision centers).

Major digital events in this decade:

– 1993: less than 100 websites were available on the internet;

– 1996: over 100,000 websites were available on the internet;

– 1998: Google was born (less than 10,000 queries a day), the digital revolution was on its way;

– 1999: a little over 50 million users were connected to the internet.

I.2.2. *Between 2000 and 2010 (the boom of e-commerce, then the advent of social networks)*

In the early 2000s, the "Web" joined the dance of Business Intelligence and "Web Analytics" was created. For the first time, consumer buying behavior could be analyzed through a sales dialogue automated by software agents: e-commerce sites (all events could be captured and analyzed by those who knew how to use decision-making solutions). More than an evolution, this was a revolution in the true sense of the word: marketing departments rushed to this mine full of data and "Web Analytics" was born (showing the very beginnings of Big Data in the volume and new structures of the data). The technical problems differed slightly. We started to talk about transactional data (mostly navigation) that had little structure or was not structured at all (the data contained in logs: trace files in e-commerce applications). It was therefore necessary to develop processes to structure the data on each page (in websites); TAGs (see Glossary) appeared, structuring web data to feed Web Analytics solutions while users surfed the web.

At the same time (drawing on businesses' increasing maturity in this domain), business departments were taking more and more control over their data and decision support tools: competency centers (business experts with knowledge in business processes, decision-making data and tools) were implemented and BICCs were born. We could now start to talk about Business Intelligence (which could manifest as business departments taking decision-making solutions, which are "simplified" in terms of implementation and usage to improve their knowledge); the world of decision-making became "Business-centric" and information became increasingly available throughout the business. Information was being "democratized" and nothing would stop it.

The mid-2000s saw the emergence of "Operational" Business Intelligence. Temporality is the key to this approach and the guiding principle is that the decision must be taken close to its implementation (action). Operational departments operated performance indicators, etc. in almost real-time using "operation" Business Intelligence solutions (dashboards with data updated in almost real-time) which were part of their business process. The democratization of information was accelerating!

Major digital events in this decade:

– 2004: Facebook, the birth of a global social network;

– 2007: the iPhone was launched; smartphones were brought out of the professional sphere;

– 2007: over 1.2 billion Google queries a day;

– 2010: over 1.5 billion users connect to the Internet (30 times more than 10 years before).

I.2.3. *Since 2010 (mobility and real-time become keywords)*

The explosion of smartphones and tablets at the end of the decade marked a radical change in the way we looked at activity monitoring (and therefore Business Intelligence and associated tools) and the relationship between businesses and their clients. Mobility became the keyword, and we began living in a "connected" world (correct information, in the correct sequence, at the correct time, for the correct person, but also on the correct device – PC, tablet, smartphone – wherever the location). The acceleration of the availability of data (whether it is to monitor/optimize the activity or the relationship between the business and their client) confirms the need for decision-making and action processes to be automated (by delegating these tasks to software agents: "human" structures can no longer cope with them). We are going to see the spread (mostly online) of solutions inside e-commerce sites, of real-time rule and analysis engines that can act and react in the transitional cycle at the customer session level (in terms of the internet, a session is a sequence containing the set of exchanges between the internet user and the website), taking into account context (the where and what), the moment (the when), and the transaction (the same action that earlier or later could have/could give a different result).

Following the launch of tablets, such as the IPad, in addition to the proliferation of smartphones, Business Intelligence solutions must be able to adapt their publication content to different presentation formats (Responsive/Adaptive Design, see Glossary).

Major digital events in this decade:

– 2010: the iPad was launched;

– 2012: over 3 billion Google queries a day;

– 2012: over 650 million websites online;

– 2013: over 2.5 billion users connect to the internet;

– 2014: over 1.3 billion Facebook accounts.

I.2.4. *And then ... (connected objects...)*

Looking forward five years from now (to 2020), what could (will) happen?

– the number of internet users will continue to grow;

– social networks (Facebook, Twitter, etc.) will continue to grow;

– new devices ("Google glasses" or "lenses", etc.) with new uses will be created, such as augmented reality which enables information to be added to visual elements (like the route to an office in a place we do not know);

– everyday objects will be connected to the internet, and they will have new uses and associated services (domotics might really take off, as well as other domains such as medical telediagnosis, and many more);

– internet users will imagine/invent new uses from technologies that are made available to them (and businesses will have to adapt).

As a consequence, the volume of available data (see Figure 1.2, IDC analysis of this exponential growth) will "explode". This data will be the raw material required for implementing these new services; it will be processed in real time (by software agents, recommendation engines) and the internet will be more than ever, the nerve center of this activity.

I.3. In sum

Our world is becoming more digitalized every day. Information technologies are causing this digitalization; data ("Big" or not) are the vectors. Businesses that are currently struggling to process the volume, format and speed of their data, and/or that do not have the structures to take value from it, can expect to be overwhelmed (or even find it impossible to take advantage of new opportunities) in the very near future. What is difficult today in terms of "data management" will be worse tomorrow for anyone who is not prepared.

1

What is Big Data?

1) A "marketing" approach derived from technology that the information technologies (IT) industry (and its associated players) comes up on a regular basis.

2) A reality we felt coming for a long time in the world of business (mostly linked to the growth of the Internet), but that did not yet have a name.

3) The formalization of a phenomenon that has existed for many years, but that has intensified with the growing digitalization of our world.

The answer is undoubtedly all three at the same time. The volume of available data continues to grow, and it grows in different formats, whereas the cost of storage continues to fall (see Figure 1.1), making it very simple to store large quantities of data. Processing this data (its volume and its format), however, is another problem altogether. Big Data (in its technical approach) is concerned with data processing; Smart Data is concerned with analysis, value and integrating Big Data into business decision-making processes.

Big Data should be seen as new data sources that the business needs to integrate and correlate with the data it already has, and not as a concept (and its associated solutions) that seeks to replace Business Intelligence (BI). Big Data is an addition to and completes the range of solutions businesses have implemented for data processing, use and distribution to shed light on their decision-making, whether it is for strategic or operational ends.

Figure 1.1. *In 1980, 20 GB of storing space weighed 1.5 tons and cost $1M; today 32 GB weighs 20 g and costs less than €20*

Technological evolutions have opened up new horizons for data storage and management, enabling anything and everything to be stored at a highly competitive price (taking into account the volume and the fact the data have very little structure, such as photographs, videos, etc.). A greater difficulty is getting value from this data, due to the "noise" generated by the data that has not been processed prior to the storage process (too much data "kills" data); this is a disadvantage. A benefit, however, is that "raw" data storage opens (or at least does not close) the door to making new discoveries from "source" data. This would not have been possible if the data had been processed and filtered before storage. It is therefore a good idea to arbitrate between these two axes, following the objectives that will have been set.

1.1. The four "V"s characterizing Big Data

Big Data is the "data" principally characterized by the four "V"s. They are Volume, Variety, Velocity and Value (associated with Smart Data).

1.1.1. *V for "Volume"*

In 2014, three billion Internet users connected to the Internet using over six billion objects (which are mainly servers, personal computers (PCs), tablets and smartphones) using an Internet Protocol (IP) address (a "unique" identifier that enables a connected object to be uniquely identified and therefore to enable communication with its peers, which are mainly smartphones, tablets and computers). This generated about eight exabytes (10 to the power of 18 = a billion) for 2014 alone. A byte is a sequence of eight bits (the bit is the basic unit in IT, represented by zero or one) and enables information to be digitalized. In the very near future (see Figure 1.2) and with the advent of connected objects (everyday objects such as televisions, domestic appliances and security cameras that will be connected to the Internet), it is predicted that there will be several tens of billions. We are talking somewhere in the region of 50 billion, which will be able to generate more than 40,000 exabytes (40,000 billion of billion bytes) of data a year. The Internet is, after all, full of words and billions of events occur every minute. Some may have value for or be relevant to a business, others less so. Therefore, to find out which have value, it is necessary to read them, sort them, in short, "reduce" the data by sending the data through a storage, filtering, organization and then analysis zone (see section 1.2).

The Digital Universe: exponential growth of digital data between 2010 and 2020

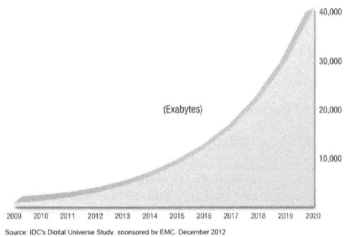

Source: IDC's Digital Universe Study, sponsored by EMC. December 2012

Figure 1.2. *Research by the IDC on the evolution of digital data between 2010 and 2020 (source: http://www.emc.com/collateral/ analyst-reports/idc-the-digital-universe-in-2020.pdf)*

The main reason for this exponential evolution will be connected objects. We expect there to be approximately 400 times the current annual volume in 2020.

1.1.2. V for "Variety"

For a long time, we only processed data that had a good structure, often from transaction systems. Once the data had been extracted and transformed, it was put into what are called decision-support databases. These databases differ from others by the data model (the way data are stored and the relationships between data):

– Transaction data model:

This model (structure of data storage and management) focuses on the execution speed of reading, writing and data modification actions to minimize the duration of a transaction to the lowest possible time (response time) and maximize the number of actions that can be conducted in parallel (scalability, e.g. an e-commerce site must be able to support thousands of Internet users who simultaneously access a catalog containing the products available and their prices via very selective criteria, which require little or no access to historical data). In this case, it is defined as a "normalized" data model, which organizes data structures into types, entities (e.g. client data are stored in a different structure to product data, invoice data, etc.), resulting in little or no data redundancy. In contrast, during the data query, we have to manage the countless and often complex, relations, joints between these entities (excellent knowledge of the data model is required, and these actions are delegated to solutions and applications and are very scarcely executed by a business analyst as they are much too complex).

In sum, the normalized model enables transaction activities to run efficiently, but makes implementing BI solutions and operational reporting (little or no space for analysis) difficult to implement directly on the transactional data model. To mitigate this issue, the operational data store (ODS) was put in place to implement some of the data tables (sourced from the transactional database) to an operational reporting database, with a more simple (light) data model. BI tools enabled a semantic layer (metadata) to be implemented, signaling a shift from a technical to a business view of the data, thereby allowing analysts to create reports without any knowledge of the physical data model.

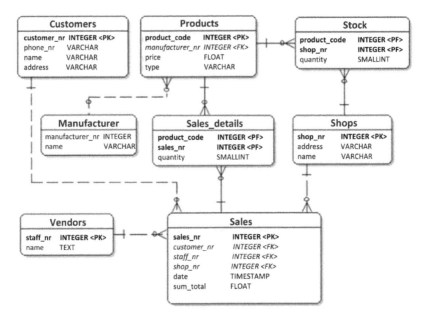

Figure 1.3. *(Normalized) transaction data model*

– Decision data model:

This model focuses on analysis, modeling, data mining, etc., which, the majority of the time, require a large volume of historic information: several years with much broader data access criteria (e.g. all products for all seasons). These restrictions have made the use of relational data models difficult, if not impossible (joints and relations between entities, associated with volume, had a huge impact on the execution time of queries). As a solution to this problem, denormalized data models were implemented. The structure of these models is much simpler (they are known as "star" or "snowflake" models, corresponding to the set of stars connected by their dimensions), where source data are stored in one structure containing all entities, for instance the client, the product, the price and the invoice are stored in the same table (known as a fact table), and can be accessed via analytical dimensions (such as the time, the customer, the product name, the location, etc.), giving the structure a star shape (hence the name of the model). This data model facilitates access (it has little or no joints beyond those necessary for dimension tables) and this access is much more sequential (though indexed). Conversely, there is a redundancy of data caused by the method information is stored in the "fact" table (there is therefore a larger volume to process).

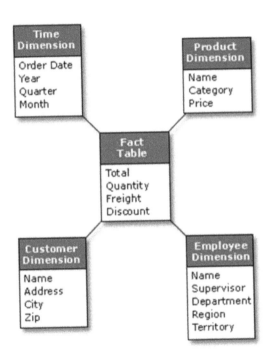

Figure 1.4. *"Star" data model (decision, denormalized)*

For several years, businesses have had to deal with data that are much less structured (or not structured at all, see

Figure 1.5), such as messaging services, blogs, social networks, Web logs, films, photos, etc. These new types of data have to be processed in a particular way (classification, MapReduce, etc.) so that they can be integrated into business decision-making solutions.

Figure 1.5. *Visual News study from 2012 gives an idea of the volume and format of data created every minute online (source: http://www. visualnews.com/ 2012/06/19/how-much-data-created-every-minute)*

1.1.3. V for "Velocity"

The Internet and its billions of users generate uninterrupted activity (the Internet never sleeps). All these activities (whether they are commercial, social, cultural, etc.) are generated by software agents – e-commerce sites, blogs, social networks, etc. – who produce continuous flows of data. Businesses must be able to process this data in "real time".

The term "real time" is still proving difficulty to define. In the context of the Internet, it could be said that this time must be aligned to the temporality of the user's session. Businesses must be able to act and react (offer content, products, prices, etc., in line with their clients' expectations, regardless of the time of day or night) in the extremely competitive context that is the Internet. A client does not belong (or no longer belongs) to one business or brand and the notion of loyalty is becoming increasingly blurred. Businesses and brands will only have a relationship with a client for as long as the client wants one and, in these conditions, meeting expectations every time is a must.

1.1.4. V for "Value", associated with Smart Data

1.1.4.1. What value can be taken from Big Data?

This question is the heart of this topic/subject: the value of Big Data is the value of every piece of data. It could be said that one piece of data that would never have any value (and that would never be used in any way) will be reduced to a piece of data that has a cost (for its processing, storage, etc.). A piece of data therefore finds its value in its use. Businesses are well aware that they are far from using all the data at their disposition (they are primarily focused on well-structured data from transaction systems). Globalization associated with the (inflationist) digitalization of our world has highlighted this awareness: competition has become tougher, there are more opportunities and the ability of "knowing" before acting is a real advantage. Big Data follows the same value rule: it must be seen as an additional source of information (structured and unstructured) that will enrich businesses' decision-making processes (both technical and human). It is from this "melting pot" that Big Data starts its transformation into Smart Data (see Chapter 2).

The example below (Figure 1.6) shows the results of an analysis into the number of tweets posted about the price of rice in Indonesia (it can easily be supposed that they are linked to purchases) and the price of rice itself (which is correlated with the tweet curve). Buyers with real-time access to this information will undoubtedly have an advantage (to be able to buy at the right moment, when the price is at its lowest) over others who do not.

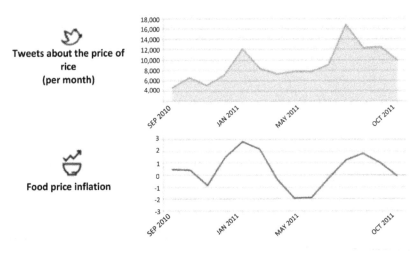

Figure 1.6. *UN Global Pulse study from 2012: correlation in Indonesia between tweets about the price of rice and the sale price of rice [UNI 14]*

Another valuable example is "cognitive business", that is Web players' (such as Google, Facebook, etc., which provide a certain number of free services for their users) ability to analyze the data they manage and store (provided to them free of charge by Internet users) to produce and sell it to economic players (information relevant to their activities).

1.2. The technology that supports Big Data

The technology was launched by Google (in 2004) to process huge volumes of data (billions of queries are made online every day on search engines). The technology was inspired by massively parallel processing solutions (MapReduce) used for large scientific calculations. The principle was to parallelize data processing by distributing it over hundreds (and even thousands) of servers (Hadoop Distributed File System) organized into processing nodes. Apache (Open Source) seized the concept and developed it into what we know today.

MapReduce is a set of data distribution processes and processing over a large number of servers (guaranteed by the "Map" process to ensure parallel processing). Results are consolidated (ensured by the "Reduce" process) to then feed the analytical follow-up where this information is analyzed and consolidated to enrich decision-making processes (either human or automated).

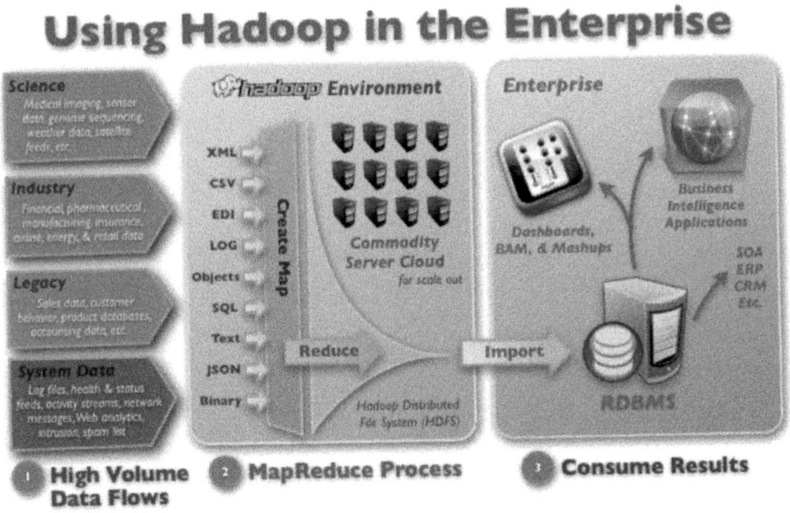

Figure 1.7. *Hadoop process & MapReduce*

What is Smart Data?

2.1. How can we define it?

Smart Data is the way in which different data sources (including Big Data) are brought together, correlated, analyzed, etc., to be able to feed decision-making and action processes. Lots of data are "Big" (in terms of volume, velocity, etc.) but how much is "Smart", that is, has value for the business?

Smart Data should be seen as a set of technologies and processes, as well as the structures associated with it (Business Intelligence Competency Centers (BICCs)) that enable all value to the taken from the data. It arises from BI.

Smart Data is one of the foundations of BI (either analytic or operational) that has evolved through BI "2.0" toward a certain number of new characteristics as follows.

2.1.1. *More formal integration into business processes*

Integrated into the heart of business processes (necessary information is distributed to all levels of the business), decision-making must be as close as possible to its implementation (action). The monitoring and optimization indicators of the activity are aligned to the operational decision-making and action processes. Operational departments have been fast to adopt this new generation of tools whose approach is more operational than analytical. It is thus simpler to align business monitoring through common and measurable indicators and objectives (see Key Performance Indicators (KPI)). Structures around BI aligned themselves with this approach by becoming more cross-functional, and BICCs appeared. Globalization, which has led to the decentralization of decision-making centers, and the fast-paced digitalization of our environment require distributed and zero latency decision-making and action processes.

2.1.2. A stronger relationship with transaction solutions

The Internet has changed data in terms of the decision-making and action cycle. The digitalization of transaction processes (e-commerce sites, etc.) has facilitated the integration and the communication between the worlds of transactions (space for operational activities) and decision-making (space for analytical activities). This stronger relationship required the duration of the "decision-making" cycle – composed of capturing and transforming data, storage and analysis, publication – to be drastically reduced to feed the decision-making and action cycle.

A few examples in support of this:

– Recommendation engines appeared on e-commerce sites. These software agents interact in real time (in the context of the Internet user's session) on the basis of statistical analysis, improved by the transaction context, to make recommendations (different products, prices, etc., can be offered following the Internet user's browsing or from a knowledge of his or her preferences) within the transaction process itself. The recommendation engine implements its rules by the:

- analytical data of segmentations, scores, appetency, etc.;

- transaction data of context, browsing, etc.

– Alerts about events: it is easy to receive notifications about whether this or that event took place (such as tracking a delivery step-by-step) and even to automate a certain number of actions linked to this event.

– In terms of payment security, using fraud detection risk algorithms (self-learning), it is possible to validate or invalidate a purchase in real time via a credit card (limiting a business' risk of debt).

In these examples, transaction events have moved closer to decision-making data, and all via rules/recommendation engines.

2.1.3. *The mobility and the temporality of information*

New devices, such as tablets or smartphones, associated with increasingly well-performing networks (wireless fidelity (WiFi), 4G), which through an almost permanent connection to the Internet (or internal business networks) via wireless communications, have become the key vectors for this new "information space–time". The link between information and those consuming it (strategic or operational decision makers or Internet users) is never interrupted (making it possible to find the right information, at the right moment, in the right context for the right decision). Information has had to adapt to these new formats (the advent of "responsive/adaptive design" or the ability of information content to adapt to the technical presentation restrictions of different devices). The temporality of data processing processes (data capture, data analysis and data restitution) has been aligned with the temporality of business processes, for which the information is destined (this point is crucial as it requires a good knowledge of business processes). This new way of working required the information system (IS) to evolve, to be urbanized (managing the communication between the IS's components) so that the information can be processed in "real time". This IS urbanization model is known as event-driven architecture (EDA), and its aim is to "urbanize" data toward the systems consuming it in almost real time.

2.1.3.1. *The automation of analysis*

The Internet never sleeps (online activity is permanent as it is always daytime somewhere on the planet). Analysis tools and cycles have had to adapt to this new temporality. Historically, businesses used the "non-active" period, generally nighttime, to process data and update decision support systems, whereas the Internet has made this way of working less effective and sometimes not effective at all. Data analysis, modeling, segmentation, etc., processes have been automated. They have become self-learning – they can integrate the new information they receive bit by bit – so they can then be used by transaction applications (rules and recommendation engines, etc.), which split analytical processes into:

– operational analysis (to support transaction solutions) is characterized by automated "operational" analytical processing. Human intervention is limited to controlling and monitoring the correct application of rules and/or the coherence of models via tools integrated into the analytical platform. Transaction information (such as visits to Webpages, consultations of products/prices, purchases, etc.) gradually improves databases, models, etc., used by rules engines and recommendation engines;

– exploratory analysis (place for construction, research, etc.) is a more traditional analysis method in which analysts/statisticians analyze data with the aim of learning new things to improve operational analysis.

These two methods are complementary. Exploratory analysis (analytical) discovers and builds models (for instance purchasing behavior, client segmentation, appetency scores, etc.) that will then be used (in real time) and improved during operational analysis.

2.2. The structural dimension

To be able to implement and use Big and Smart Data, businesses must preferably be equipped with a suitable BI structure whose function is to implement and support the company's BI strategy. BICCs are such structures.

2.2.1. *The objectives of a BICC*

1) To be a cross-functional organizational structure (to put an end to the silo approach to needs and decision-making solutions within a business) that encompasses three types of profiles:

– technical profiles that handle:

- technology (tools, databases) in terms of implementation and support;

- data quality (managing extract, transform and load (ETL) processing);

– analytical profiles that handle:

- the analysis and transcription of business needs via data analysis;

- business handover in data analysis;

– business profiles that handle:

- the link with company strategy and associated decision-making needs;

- the alignment (of processes and organization) between indicators and business processes;

- the management of change (linked to new tools, processes, etc.).

2) To implement and monitor the company's BI master plan:

– to implement a long-term road map in line with the business' (operational and strategic) needs;

– to anticipate developments around BI (tools, new trends, etc.) by implementing a BI awareness group.

3) To optimize investments around decision-making projects:

– to ensure the coherence of BI projects, pool resources (techniques and human);

– to implement and monitor a data governance program;

– to define the company's BI norms and standards;

– to train users in terms of both tools and data.

2.3. The closed loop between Big Data and Smart Data

Figure 2.1 shows the relationship between Big Data and Smart Data through two main axes: knowledge (*in fine* the value of information) and velocity (the temporality, update frequency). The value (knowledge) that can be taken from a piece of information that is very fast (reflecting an almost immediate reality) and that can only be contextualized a little or not at all is without doubt weak if not useless. Likewise, a piece of information that is very well contextualized but that is not well updated or not updated at all does not reflect or no longer reflects reality. Putting these two dimensions together and creating a closed loop between Big Data and Smart Data enabled this problem to be avoided.

Big Data produces large volumes of transaction data (purchasing activity, Web site browsing, etc.) very quickly (almost in real time). To avoid this velocity being altered, data processing must be limited. It is difficult, over the course of a few short seconds, to capture, process and model browsing data from an e-commerce site with thousands of connected users, and then interact in real time (in the context of the user's session) to make recommendations. In contrast, extracting data necessary for the real time contextualization (e.g. country of origin, previously consulted pages/products, number of visits via cookies and/or TAGS on the page) of browsing (transaction by transaction) enables recommendation processes, rules management, etc., to retrieve the correct information (behavior/purchasing models, client segment, etc.) from Smart Data to optimize its actions (e.g. recommend an alternative product).

The example below (Figure 2.1) illustrates the "real-time" monitoring of the sales process activity (volume of purchase transactions per hour). "Smart Data" will enable us (from a decision-making database in which historic sales transactions are integrated) to construct a model (the solid curve in the figure below) that predicts sales activity for an equivalent day (same seasons, day of the week, etc.), whereas "Big Data" will capture in real time the sales activity (dotted curve in the figure below). It can be clearly seen that bringing these two pieces of information together enables the activity to be monitored (the model represented by the solid curve as the objective, whereas the other doted curve represents a reality).

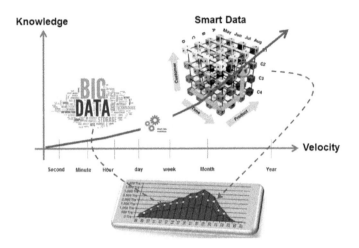

Figure 2.1. *From Big Data to Smart Data, a closed loop*

The solid curve is the analytical model use to predict the predicting, where the dotted curve shows the real time activity.

Zero Latency Organization

3.1. From Big Data to Smart Data for a zero latency organization

A zero latency organization is best described as an organization whose temporality of activity monitoring, via the implementation of its decisions (human actions or software agents), is directly linked to the temporality of its business processes in order to respond as fast as possible to changes in context (based on the idea that it is necessary to know to be able to decide, and to decide to be able to act).

3.2. Three types of latency

3.2.1. *Latency linked to data*

Latency linked to data could be deemed "technical" as it is directly linked to the architecture and the urbanization of the information system (this book will not develop these concepts, but they widely represent the "technical" aspects of the information system and the communication modalities between its components). The objective is to "capture" transaction data, the moment it is generated without disturbing the transaction cycle (response time). This type of information system architecture is said to be event-driven (event-driven architecture (EDA)). Once the data has been captured, it must be urbanized: the data is processed ("mapped", filtered, etc.) such that it can be used as input for analytical processing. Implementing an EDA architecture can be costly and very intrusive for solutions that are already in place. The most pragmatic approach is to see what can be realized (using the current Information System) in terms of "capturing" and "urbanizing" the data (granularity, temporality, etc.) and to adjust the temporality of the activity monitoring to these constraints on the basis of the existing architecture and solutions (this is an important step that validates the approach in terms of its working capacity and value).

3.2.2. *Latency linked to analytical processes*

This type of latency is attributed to the "analytical" processing of data. It consists of contextualizing the transaction data (from Big Data) using decision-making data (to Smart Data), which is then "consumed":

– by decision makers (either strategic or operational) using dashboards that are available on different devices such as personal computers, smartphones or tablets;

– by rule and/or recommendation engines, for all automated processing (often used for e-commerce sites).

These two types of latency (data and analytical) are known as "data latency" and are primarily addressed by IT solutions (which are currently in place or that will be developed). Costs (mostly IT) related to reducing this latency can be very high and can only be justified by the capacity decision makers (strategic or operational) will have in monitoring and optimizing their processes. Therefore, it is important, before committing oneself, to have checked business departments' ability to integrate the information and the associated temporality in monitoring and optimizing their activities (and therein deliver the value).

3.2.3. *Latency linked to decision-making processes*

This type of latency relates to business; the determining factor is the capacity, and particularly the temporality, decision makers (or a delegated automated process) require to implement actions linked to their decision-making. This latency is directly linked to target business processes and associated organizations, and/or to a set of automated processes. In all cases, this type of latency must be seen as the first constraint to be analyzed while the solution is being implemented. The latency of the data must be aligned to this constraint or objective. This step is decisive in the choice of which architecture and technical solutions will be implemented, and by capillarity, the costs and the schedule (duration) of the project.

3.2.4. *Action latency*

Action latency corresponds to the sum of: data latency (primarily technological latency) + the latency of decision-making and action processes (primarily structural latency).

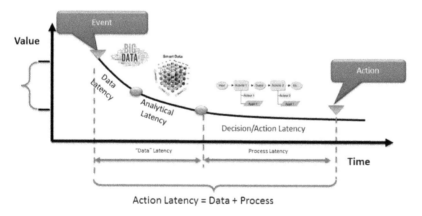

Figure 3.1. *The three types of latency*

4

Summary by Example

This chapter will back up the assertions made previously by describing three examples of solutions that have been implemented in real life.

The aim is to follow the key stages of a purchasing cycle (on an e-commerce platform) and the consumption of a trip away.

The first step will be to discover what is on offer (products, services, price, etc.) on an e-commerce platform where decision-making and action processes have been automated by a recommendation engine, which deals with the customer's needs and the associated responses. The processes have been automated to make the customer the best offer possible (taking into account the arrival date, the length of stay, location, etc.) in addition to a certain number of alternative offers which are determined by their customer profile in the event a user is surfing "anonymously" (without logging into a customer account) on the e-commerce site.

The second step is the purchase action, again on an e-commerce platform, that is subjected to price and offer availability constraints. Available stock is updated in "real time", and thus enables or prevents the sale of certain products/prices. This is revenue optimization in the context of selling services (such as a hotel room or transport) and is known as "Yield Management".

The final step is the use of the service (in our example, a tourist trip) via the optimization of operational performance, which at each stage of the trip will have a direct impact on customer experience.

4.1. Example 1: date/product/price recommendation

In the context of hotel bookings optimization, demand is seasonal (see Figure 4.1). Demand is higher at weekends – guests arriving on Friday or Saturday (demand sometimes exceeds the physical capacity of the hotel) – than it is on weekdays (guests arriving Sunday to Thursday). A way to reduce seasonality would be to shift excess demand at the weekend to fill the lack of demand on weekdays.

Our analysis determined that there are two (structural) types of customer profile:

– date sensitive: customers who do not have the option (nor the desire) to visit outside of the dates they chose (for example, the weekend or school holidays);

– price sensitive: customers who would change the date of their stay (to a weekday or a different period) if the price or associated services were "appealing".

The figure clearly shows that there is an excess of demand on the weekend (denied demand), whereas there is a shortfall on weekdays (free capacity). The aim is to shift (while controlling the risk of cannibalization) the denied demand toward the free capacity in order to limit the seasonality of demand and then, *in fine*, optimize assets (revenue, margin, etc.).

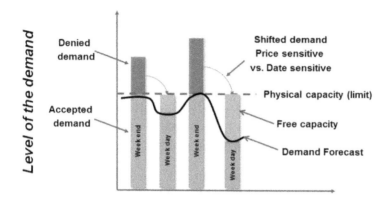

Date (seasonality)

Figure 4.1. *Resolving the problem of the seasonality of demand*

The solution selected (see Figure 4.2) was to bring together two worlds: the transaction world, via the e-commerce platform, and the decision-making world, represented by Big Data and Smart Data.

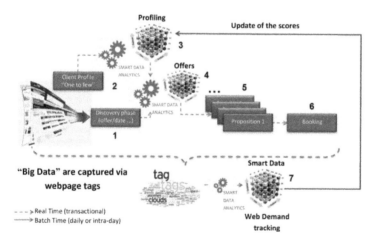

Figure 4.2. *Implemented solution to manage the seasonality of demand in the transaction process and in the context of "anonymous" customers (who do not have a personal account on the platform, which would enable them to be identified and thus categorized)*

The process, step-by-step (see step numbers in Figure 4.2), are detailed in the following.

4.1.1. *Steps "1" and "2"*

The first two steps fall well and truly into the world of "Big Data" as they have a high velocity of data that are not very structured or not structured at all.

This is a discovery phase. On the one hand, the Internet users will discover the products, prices, etc. and, on the other hand, the system will capture (via TAGs placed on the pages of the e-commerce site) the key information requiring "segmentation" (defining the Internet user profile, in the marketing sense of the term). The aim is, on the basis of this information, to be able to suggest, via a recommendation engine, offers that are "compatible" with their expectations (trips, dates, price, etc.).

There are two types of key information for this process:

– declarative information (provided by the user):

  - the *where*: the choice of the destination;

  - the *when*: the date of arrival;

  - the *how long*: the duration of the trip;

  - the *for whom*: the composition of participants (number of adults and children).

This information will be used as input in recommendation engines to index all the "eligible" products for sale, responding to user criteria.

– information surmised from surfing (provided by TAGs placed on the pages of the e-commerce site):

  - the source of the traffic (where the Internet user comes from; from a research engine, a commercial redirected link, etc.);

- the type of device used by the Internet user (if the surfer is using a Smartphone, the content and particularly the number of alternatives has to be adapted versus a PC where there is more space for the presentation);

- the country of origin (for instance, to propose offers involving transport, etc.).

The recommendation engines use these two types of (contextual) information for the remainder of the process.

4.1.2. Steps "3" and "4": enter the world of "Smart Data"

The recommendation engine takes over. Using the contextual information (steps 1 and 2), it indexes "Smart Data", that is the Internet user profile and the products (taken from a list of eligible products) the user will be offered, feeding the next step.

4.1.3. Step "5": the presentation phase

This step enables the offers to be presented in context and according to a certain number of configurable presentation criteria (number of responses, etc.):

– *offer 1* is an offer of a trip/price that corresponds (according to the availabilty of the offer for this date) to the Internet user's initial demand;

– *offer 2* is the first "alternative" offer of date or destination (which is more appealing in terms of price and/or services), which might correspond to the user profile. The objectivie is to shift demand toward a date where there is higher availability (for instance, a trip during the week rather than at the weekend);

– *offer 3* is the second "alternative" offer that may take other criteria into account (such as the increased number of products in the customer's basket), by offering rates equivalent to offer 1 but including more services;

– *N offer*: the Nth "alternative" (connected to the distribution strategy of the business and which has the presentation capacity of the e-commerce platform).

This cycle can be repeated by the user as many times as necessary. All these steps must be executed in several seconds so that there is no impact on the customer experience. The time it takes to refresh pages and their content is a key factor at the core of the sales dialogue; this time must be minimized so as to maintain interaction with the user.

4.1.4. Step "6": the "Holy Grail" (the purchase)

The sales dialogue (potentially) continues with purchase and payment. The data from step 6 correlated with the data from step 5 enable the system to segment customers into:

– "price" or service sensitive customers:

- i.e. customers who accepted one of the alternative offers.

– "date" sensitive customers:

- i.e. customers who despite the alternative offers opted for an offer corresponding to their initial date, trip, etc. criteria.

4.1.5. Step "7": Smart Data

This step consists of processing and consolidating the transaction information collected throughout the day in order to improve Smart Data. It enables models, scores, etc.

to be updated (the system becomes self-learning) to then feed the recommendation engine.

This is a textbook example of the transaction and the decision-making worlds being brought together, creating a closed loop between Big Data and Smart Data. This partnership relies on software agents (to which decision-making and action processes were delegated), primarily the recommendation engine.

4.2. Example 2: yield/revenue management (rate controls)

Yield or revenue management is the management of a perishable, in other words, non-storable asset or service, such as plane tickets, hotel rooms, etc. (for a given date or journey). Businesses pay a price when these assets or services are not sold (e.g. on a given date the plane will take off with empty seats or the hotel will have empty rooms, etc.).

The two main objectives of yield/revenue management are:

– to ensure hotel rooms, plane tickets, etc., are filled when *demand does not exceed capacity*. This means finding a good balance between price and service (related to marketing), in comparison to the market price such as to stimulate demand;

– to optimize revenue/margin when *demand exceeds available capacity*. Each and every one of us will have noticed at some point that the price of services such as journeys, plane tickets, etc., follows a certain seasonality (most pricey in holiday periods where there is strong demand and the seats, rooms, etc., will certainly be filled versus other periods in the year where some planes take off with empty seats). These "fluctuations" are managed by yield management solutions.

In more technical terms, yield/revenue management can be defined as a technique for forecasting demand (for all available rates) without constraint. The term "without constraint" means a context of limitless capacity (in the plane example, this would mean we had a virtual plane containing as many available seats as people wanting to travel on the date in question). The constraint is then "filtered" (the real capacity of the plane) in order to allocate capacity (plane seats) in decreasing price order (from highest to lowest).

For example, in a context where there are three available rates for a given flight and date:

– rate 1 = 100€:

  - forecasted demand without constraint: 200.

– rate 2 = 80€ (20% discount):

  - forecasted demand without constraint: 150.

– rate 3 = 70€ (30% discount):

  - forecasted demand without constraint: 100.

which gives a total demand without constraint of 450 seats.

The real capacity of the plane is 240 seats; there is, therefore, a difference of 210 seats (in comparison with demand without constraint). Optimization consists of maximizing revenue by "controlling" the quantity of seats to be allocated (made available for sale) by rate. In this example, rate 3 (–30%) will not be available for sale for this flight for this date (since there is enough demand for higher rates to fill the plane), whereas rate 2 (–20%) will be limited to 40 seats (+ or – the reliability/probability of the forecast, but let us consider a definite scenario) and the large majority of seats (200) will be reserved for rate 1 (no discount). Optimization will produce as output a certain number of rate controls that will have to be interpreted by the distribution system (and therefore sales system).

This control step is realized on sales systems (where decision-making meets the transaction). These controls come in the form of a bid price (or price floor, which closes offers, see Figure 4.3). In a sales context (a service, a date, remaining stock, etc.), the bid price can be seen as a long list of thresholds indexed according to remaining available stock. When there is less stock, the low rates are closed and vice versa (based on the principle of "what is rare is expensive"). The resulting bid price will serve as the basis for opening (if the rate is >= than the bid price) or closing (if the rate is < than the bid price) the available rates in the context, in order to optimize the revenue generated by the sale of the good or service. The forecasting dimension (enabling an evaluation of the demand for a service to be conducted) belongs to the activity of each business and is directly linked to the markets targeted by the business.

The solutions supporting yield management are analytical (decision-making) and rely on demand modeling techniques (of the natural demand of the consumer, which is captured and then analyzed even before price/availability is validated). Their aim is to forecast demand without constraint (by date, service, market segment, etc.), which will then feed the constrained optimization module (e.g. limited stock/inventory), whose task it is to calculate the bid price (for the combination of service/date/state of stock). Let us consider the example of a regular (daily) flight from Paris to New York, on a plane with a capacity of 500 seats, and tickets that can be purchased up to one year in advance (365 days). The bid price table would be: 500 (seats) × 365 days (one year) = 182,500 check-ins (for one flight, large airlines operate several hundreds of flights, if not thousands).

The table will be indexed during the sale transaction process according to date and the remaining inventory and stock for sale			The bid price acts as a threshold for ticket price
Stock/index	Inventory	Date	Bid price €
0	Paris-New York	01/01/2015	800
1	Paris-New York	01/01/2015	800
2	Paris-New York	01/01/2015	800
3	Paris-New York	01/01/2015	750
...	Paris-New York	01/01/2015	...
50	Paris-New York	01/01/2015	600
...	Paris-New York	01/01/2015	...
500	Paris-New York	01/01/2015	400

Table 4.1. *If 50 seats are still available, with a bid price of 600€, all the offers with expected revenues < bid price will be closed*

This example clearly shows that the more stock remains, the lower the bid price (enabling access to lower ticket prices). The bid price is inversely proportional to the remaining stock.

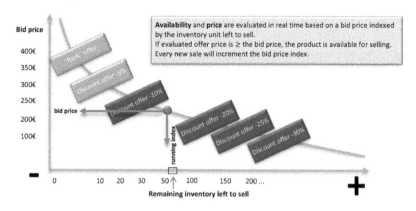

Figure 4.3. *Bid price curve*

These solutions must be "completely" integrated into the distribution system (sales: call center, web, etc.) whose task is to manage the opening or the closing of the sale of a rate (and thus the availability of a product) in "real time" via the bid price. Each time the remaining stock is updated there is an impact on the bid price: it rises if the available stock falls (following sales) and falls if the available stock increases (following cancellations). The dynamism of the process enables all opportunities to be seized in real time (reopen rates that were closed or close rates that were open).

4.2.1. *How it works: an explanation based on the Tetris principle (see Figure 4.4)*

The frame of the game represents the space constraint (for instance, the capacity of a hotel per number of rooms or of a plane per number of seats, etc.). The figures represent demand (which could be expressed in number of nights per trip or number of passengers per flight). This example will use the same figures throughout:

– the blue figures: initial demand that was met;

– the red figures: initial demand that was not met;

– the orange figures: additional demand that can be adapted.

1) The situation known as "first come first served." The first score is 74 out of 120 (max) and is thus a situation where assets are underoptimized. The principle is as follows: the first to come is first to be served, there is neither demand forecast nor allocation optimization, and demand is accepted as it comes. This example shows that (unless you are extremely lucky) it is quite unlikely that demand without control optimizes filling seats, rooms, etc. Assets are used at a rate of 60% meaning that 40% of assets are unused (which can easily be associated with a loss of revenue, the majority of which is marginal as assets are available).

2) The second score is 94 out of 120 (max). The previous demand scenario is applied (the same sequence), in addition to a logic for optimizing allocation (to limit "holes"). As a result, a free space was produced enabling demand (red) to be accepted when it had been refused (due to lack of space) in the first scenario. In this example, asset use is 78% (+21% in relation to the first scenario), which will have a direct impact on the growth of revenue.

3) The final score is 108 out of 120 (max) or 90% effectiveness (+31% from scenario 1). The principles of yield management are applied: forecasted demand is influenced by the optimization process (opening and closing certain rates on the basis of the "no constraint" demand forecast). In this example, demand is accepted according to forecasting and optimization rules whose objective is to accept demand at the correct moment, resulting in an "optimal" number of seats, rooms, etc. being filled and even liberating space for additional demand (orange).

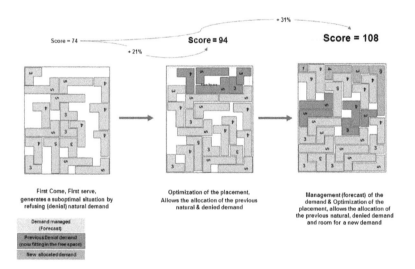

Figure 4.4. *The principle of constrained optimization, Tetris. For a color version of this figure, see www.iste.co.uk / iafrate / data.zip*

Three types of solutions were implemented. These solutions bring together the transaction world and the decision-making world:

1) *The distribution system* (the system managing offers, rates, the state of stocks and finally sales) must be able to apply controls when there is an availability/price demand for an offer. These solutions will have been produced by yield management (opening or closing rates by comparing them to the bid price during the transaction cycle in "real time": opening rates if they are > = than the bid price and closing rates if they are < than the bid price). These controls are applied when the availability of the offer in its sales context is being evaluated via an availability server (see explanation below).

2) *The availability server*'s function is to stock the bid price table (per day/inventory/capacity for each combination) and manage the distribution of availability/price for an offer (via a comparison with the current bid price) for the distribution system. Every stock action (impacting the remaining inventory) develops the indexation of the bid price table (via the left to sell a particular inventory/date) and involves a perfect synchronization between the distribution system (managing stocks and sales) and the availability server (managing the level of remaining stock and the associated bid price). If the process becomes at all desynchronized, there will be a direct impact on the offers/prices available (hence, the importance that the integration, the combination, of these two systems be of quality).

3) *The yield management system*'s (the decision-making, analytical world) function is to produce a forecast, followed by an optimization, to produce bid price tables that will be uploaded to the availability server on a daily basis (or more often, depending on how many reoptimizations are done per day).

The solution can be said to have five major steps:

1) Capturing sales by uploading data from the distribution system on a daily basis (the day before). The system then assigns a rate category which classifies the value of the sale by following the customer's basket (e.g. RC1–RC10, where RC1 has more value, followed by RC2, and so on).

2) The second step consists of aggregating and deconstraining data from step one (action consisting of simulating what demand would be if no constraint had been applied) to feed the different models (the basis of the forecast).

3) The third step is the most critical and consists of producing a demand forecast (without constraint of stock levels, closing a rate, etc.). The quality of the forecast influences the quality of the optimization (and therefore the value of the solution). It is a key step in the process.

4) This step follows optimization (resulting from the forecast). The constraint (number of seats in a plane, number of hotel rooms, etc.) is applied to demand. The (iterative) process involves allocating resources (e.g. the number of sales permitted per type of offer) to the most profitable demand. This step generates the bid price table.

5) The final step (controls) is the publication of the bid price table for the distribution system (the decision-making world feeds the transaction world).

4.3. Example 3: optimization of operational performance

This example will demonstrate how a business (in this example, a major player in the tourism industry) can be aligned and connected through its key performance indicators

(KPIs) and where (Big and Smart) "data" enables this alignment.

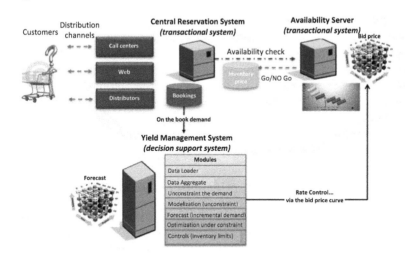

Figure 4.5. *Diagram of a conceptual architecture of an integrated yield / revenue management system*

Extract from the business' scope statement: *"To obtain a summary or detailed view of our operational activity in "real time". To provide decision-makers (both strategic and operational) with the information they need to interpret multiple and complex situations and make good decisions as close to the action as possible. The aim is to maximize customer experience, which is closely linked to the operational performance of our organization."*

The response to this scope statement was the implementation of an optimization of the operational performance, solution that is capable of processing decision-making data (activity modeling) as well as operational data (a "real time" comparison of this activity with the models, see Figure 4.6): the basis of Smart Data.

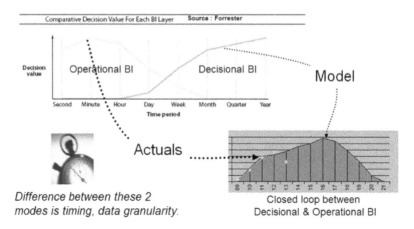

Figure 4.6. *Closed value loop between decision-making data and operational data*

Figure 4.6 compares the value cycle of data with its temporality and usage.

Decisional business intelligence (BI) implements its forecasting models on the basis of a "strong" principle: the quality of the forecast is correlated with the number of observations feeding the models. This means that the more observations of a state the business wants to forecast, the higher the quality of the forecast (standard deviation and probability). The value of these data will, therefore, grow with time (the number of past observations, such as filling hotel rooms over Christmas week). These data, which are often very detailed, will over time enable (contextualized) models to be constructed about past activities, which will then be used as the basis for demand forecasts. Creating these models and associated forecasts is a difficult (in terms of the granularity and the volume of data to be processed) and long (in terms of analytical processing) process. This meant that decisional BI was for a long time incompatible with operational requirements. Operational BI requires an almost real time temporality of the monitoring indicators for the activity and associated forecasts.

Operational BI has had the following requirement from the very start: to be able to follow the key indicators of an operational process in almost real time such as to optimize its performance. Unlike decisional BI, operational BI takes its value from temporality via people who know how to contextualize the information (the context comes from decisional BI or from the decision maker's experience, but in the latter, decisions are less based on fact and there are differences with regard to performance).

Comparing these two types of BI (loop between decisional BI and operational   BI) enabled the forecasting and optimizing of operational performances to be implemented. Its characteristics are:

– the implementation of a forecast, enabling operational decision makers to "forecast" the activities to come (for instance, a day of activities). This enabled, among others:

- the activity to be secured by anticipating actions;

- decisions to be objectivized (based on facts);

- performance to be described (or non-performance to be explained);

- etc.

– to set quantitive objectives on the basis of the forecasts;

– to be able to compare the current activity to the forecast (and therefore to the objectives) in "real time" such as to monitor the operational activity;

– every hour of the forecast is to be recalculated on the basis of contextual elements that may differ from those of the initial model (such as the real rate of visiting a restaurant versus the predicted rate), enabling the shift from "probabilistic" forecasting (linked to the probability of a forecasting model) to "constructivist" forecasting, where the model gradually adjusts to the activity.

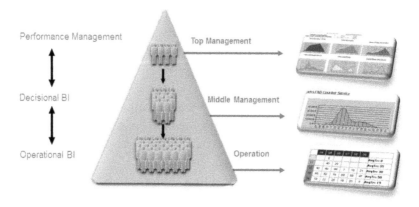

Figure 4.7. *"Connected and aligned" solutions for managing operational performance*

Figure 4.7 provides a summary of the tools that were implemented. Requirements differ for each type of population.

4.3.1. *General department (top management)*

The general department is concerned with the global (and summarized) picture of all activity across the different domains of a business' operational activity. It can "zoom in" on a particular activity domain (equivalent to dashboards in the operations department).

4.3.2. *Operations departments (middle management)*

Each operations department focuses on its domain of activities through "pictures" that span from a summary (e.g. the set of shop activity) to detailed analyses (focusing on one shop, or even a subset of one shop, such as the performance of one of the sales assistants). The aim is to be able to (quickly) identify the potential source of a malfunction (no alignment with objectives) and/or "abnormal" performance.

4.3.3. *Operations management (and operational players)*

This is the "finest" level of the analysis, such as a shop (to quote the example above). It enables operational decision makers to focus on their activity and objectives; decision makers must be able to objectivize their decisions using contextual information (what was forecast) as well as operational information (what is happening and why it is happening).

Bringing together "decision-making" and "operational" data enabled these tools to be put in place in addition to associated business processes (one does not come without the other). Figure 4.8 (operations control center) is an example of the follow-up and optimization processes of operational performance.

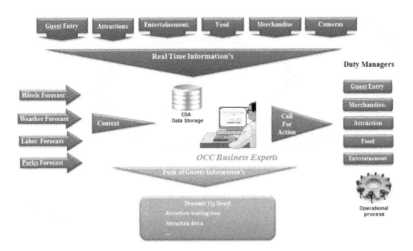

Figure 4.8. *The operations control center*

Figure 4.8 shows the structure of the follow-up and optimization of operational performance. This model is based on an operations control center (OCC) and is composed of business experts. An OCC could be compared to a "control tower" as it has a global view of the situation (in terms of indicators and images via cameras located at key points), and therefore of all the elements required to contextualize information (decision makers remain leaders of operations).

The OCC is in charge of correlating different information and communicating with operations players to inform them of:

– a performance problem within their activities;

– a wide-ranging event that may have an impact on their activities.

The different operational decision makers also have access to dashboards (related to their activities and in "real time") on their Smartphones, enabling them to follow, at all times, whether their activities are in line with their objectives, to "view" messages from the OCC, and to make decisions about what actions to take, etc.

Figure 4.9. *An example of indicators and follow-up in "real time" from call centers posted on a Smartphone*

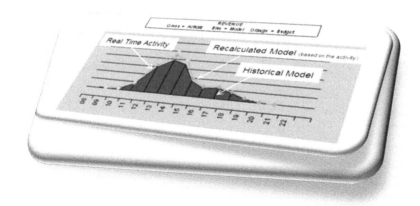

Figure 4.10. *Hour-by-hour summary of revenue follow-up for a restaurant. For a color version of this figure, see www.iste.co.uk / iafrate / data.zip*

– in blue, the analytical model from decisional BI, which produces the revenue forecast per hour for a given day;

– in green, revenue per hour, which in this example is higher than the model (perhaps due to a higher number of covers served in the restaurant between 12 pm and 2 pm than forecasted);

– in orange, the recalculated model (all hours) which considers the difference (of the hypotheses) between the initial model and the activity (blue) and reality (green). The recalculated model causes objectives to be realigned (higher or lower according to context), making the solution self-learning.

These three examples of bringing together decisional and operational   BI are solutions that have actually been implemented and have proven their value. The solutions have been completely integrated into the business operations process and it would be difficult, if not impossible, to go back.

Conclusion

Who knows what tomorrow will bring, but one thing is certain: we will be increasingly "connected". Web 2.0 started this progress; it created new needs and generated new opportunities. It is impossible to deny the (societal, political and economic) impact social networks have on our knowledge and communication society. Anybody who has a good command of these means of communication (and thus the associated data) will have an advantage over others.

Let us imagine a typical day of an entrepreneur in a perhaps not so distant future, where the majority of daily objects are "Smart" and connected.

In the morning, I am woken up by my "Smart Bed" which has calculated (from my sleep cycle) the best time for me to wake up. My "Smart Bed" communicates with my "Smart Media Hub" (stereo system, video, Internet, etc.), which connects me to my favorite Web radio as well as to my centralized control, which sets the temperature of my bathroom and the water for my shower. I then put on my "Smart Glasses or Lenses" and I am connected to the world. While eating breakfast (suggested by my virtual sports coach via my Smart Glasses), I look at a summary of what happened in the world when I was asleep (I flick through content with a simple eye movement). I look at my schedule for the day and at the same time my "Smart Fridge" asks me to order a certain number of products and suggests some associated products and promotions, which I confirm with the blink of an eye. And then I am ready to set off for a new day. I get into my "Smart Car" (which is run from renewable energy) and confirm I want the automatic driver to take me to my first meeting. In the meantime, I make a videoconference call to catch up with my team and make some final preparations for my first meeting. I arrive, my car parks itself in an energy recharging space (by induction), my "Smart Glasses" (using augmented reality) guide me to where my meeting is taking place and informs the person I am meeting of my imminent arrival. We spend the morning working on an urbanization project (I am an architect) with three-dimensional (3D) projections of different prototypes. Documents are exchanged via the "Cloud", even my computer is dematerialized, and I make all actions using my "Smart Glasses" and/or a "Smart Table" (which serves as a human–machine interface). Meanwhile, my virtual assistant tells me that she has organized some meetings for the next couple of days and asks me to confirm them, which I do with a movement on the "Smart Table" (I also could have used my "Smart Glasses"). The meeting comes to an end, I make a video-call to a friend I can see is available on the social network to arrange lunch with him. I suggest a restaurant, we access the menu and order the food as we speak. The reservation is confirmed, the coordinates are loaded into my "Smart Car", which drives me to the restaurant, where our table is waiting for us and the first dish is served several minutes after we sit down. I spend the afternoon on a collaborative job (online) with my collaborators (who are located across several continents) on the urbanization project. We confirm a prototype and materialize it with our 3D printer, ready to be presented the next day. The day comes to an end, I respond to several messages I received, including an offer (from my club) to play tennis for an hour that evening (with a player I do not know, but who has similar level to mine). I confirm the offer. I need to then stop home and my "Smart Car" chooses the optimum route. In the meantime, a "Drone" has delivered the new racquet I ordered the previous day. In the early evening, I return for a family dinner (it is 8.30 pm) and then watch a sports event connected with some friends (in which everyone can watch and replay the actions using their "Smart Glasses" from the angle they want, by connecting to one of 50 cameras that are recording the event). It is 11 pm, I receive a message from my "Smart Bed" which suggests (given my schedule for the next day) that I get 6 hours sleep. I follow its recommendation, disconnect from the virtual world and find the world of my dreams.

Bibliography

[ABU 12] ABU-MOSTAFA Y.S., MAGDON-ISMAIL M., LIN H.-T., *Learning From Data*, AMI Books, 2012.

[ALL 97] ALLAIN-DUPRE P., DUHARD N., *Les armes secrètes de la décision – La gestion de l'information au service de la performance économique,* Gualino, 1997.

[BIE 03] BIERE M., *Business Intelligence for the Enterprise (English Book)*, IBM Press, 2003.

[BUS 13] BUSINESS ANALYTIC INFO, 2013: les Big Data à la conquête de tous les métiers, available at http://business-analytics-info.fr/archives/4054/2013-les-big-data-a-la-conquete-de-tous-les-metiers/, 15 January 2013.

[CON 12] CONSTINE J., How Big Is Facebook's Data? Available at http://techcrunch.com/2012/08/22/how-big-is-facebooks-data-2-5-billion-pieces-of-content-and-500-terabytes-ingested-every-day/, 22 August 2012.

[GUM 05] GUMB B., *Une idée pour décider*, Global Village, 2005.

[KIM 03] KIMBALL R., MARGY R., *Entrepôts de données, Guide pratique de modélisation dimensionnelle*, Vuibert, 2nd ed., 2003.

[LAR 05] LAROSE D.T., *Des données à la connaissance,* translation by Thierry Vallaud, Vuibert, 2005.

[LEP 11] LEPÈRE C., MARCOUX J.-C., *Small Business Intelligence,* Edipro, Liège, 2011.

[MAR 88] MARTINET B., RIBAULT J.-M., *La Veille Technologique, Concurrentielle et Commerciale*, Editions d'Organisation, Paris, 1988.

[MAY 13] MAYER-SCHONBERGER V., CUKIER K.N., *Big Data: A Revolution That Will Transform How We Live, Work, and Think*, HMH Books, 2013.

[PER 13] PERRIN J., Big data et big brother, available at https://www.le-vpn.com/fr/big-data-et-big-brother/, accessed on 10 January 2013.

[SIN 99] SINSOU J.-P., *Yield et Revenue Management*, ITA Press, 1999.

[SMO 12] SMOLAN R., ERWITT J., *The Human Face of Big Data*, Sterling, 2012.

[UNI 14] UNITED NATIONS GLOBAL PULSE, Twitter and Perceptions of Crisis-related Stress, available at www.unglobalpulse.org/projects/twitter-and-perceptions-crisis-related-stress/, 2014.

Glossary

BI: Business Intelligence, the set of tools and structures related to the management and the use of data for operational or analytical (decision-making) purposes.

Big Data: "Raw" data of any type, which by definition exceeds the "normal" capacity of a business' data management (mostly due to the volume, velocity, variety, etc., of the data).

BICC: Business Intelligence Competency Center, an organization concerned with managing and distributing data within a business as well as BI projects.

Bid Price: Also known as the "price floor", that is the minimum revenue expected for an offer/service (used as a price limit, under which offers will not be available for sale).

Bit: Elementary computer unit representing binary information (0 or 1).

Byte: A set of eight bits, which enables information to be coded.

Data: The raw material, the element at the basis of the information cycle.

DataMART: Decision-making subject-oriented database (i.e. specialized for a certain domain, e.g. a "client" DataMART would be a decision-making database, specially designed to manage relationships with the client).

Data Warehouse: Decision-making data base containing the totality of a business' decision-making data (all subjects).

EIS: Executive Information System.

EDA: Event-driven architecture (the architecture of the information system and its urbanization that follows a model for managing and processing information according to events).

ETL: Extract Transform Load, tools and processes for data processing.

Hadoop: Set of processes and techniques for processing Big Data.

HDFS: Framework for large-scale processing and parallelized with Big Data, Hadoop Distributed File System.

KPI: Key Performance Indicators (key indicators following performance, it would be ideal if they were "interdepartmental", i.e. covered all business departments).

MapReduce: Subset of the Hadoop process that consists of filtering and consolidating Big Data.

Responsive/adaptive design: A presentation platform (e-commerce site)'s ability to adapt its content to different types of devices (PC, smartphone, tablet, etc.).

Smart Data: Data transformed into information that feeds the decision-making and action cycle.

Smart Device: Intelligent objects.

Page Tags: Technique for structuring (via code contained in the page) Web data via variables that are transmitted while the user is surfing the Web to Web Analytics solutions (where it will be processed).

Web Analytics: Business Intelligence applied to the Web (processing data of users Internet surfing, etc.).

Index

Other titles from

in

Information Systems, Web and Pervasive Computing

2014

DINET Jérôme
Information Retrieval in Digital Environments

KEMBELLEC Gérald, CHARTRON Ghislaine, SALEH Imad
Recommender Systems

VENTRE Daniel
Chinese Cybersecurity and Defense

2013

BERNIK Igor
Cybercrime and Cyberwarfare

CAPET Philippe, DELAVALLADE Thomas
Information Evaluation

LEBRATY Jean-Fabrice, LOBRE-LEBRATY Katia
Crowdsourcing: One Step Beyond

2012

GAUSSIER Eric, YVON François
Textual Information Access

STOCKINGER Peter
Audiovisual Archives: Digital Text and Discourse Analysis

VENTRE Daniel
Cyber Conflict

2011

LEMBERGER Pirmin, MOREL Mederic
managing Complexity of Information Systems

STOCKINGER Peter
Introduction to Audiovisual Archives

STOCKINGER Peter
Digital Audiovisual Archives

VENTRE Daniel
Cyberwar and Information Warfare

2010

BONNET Pierre
Enterprise Data Governance

2009

BONNET Pierre, DETAVERNIER Jean-Michel, VAUQUIER Dominique
Sustainable IT Architecture: the Progressive Way of Overhauling Information Systems with SOA

PAPY Fabrice
Information Science

RIVARD François, ABOU HARB Georges, MERET Philippe
The Transverse Information System

VENTRE Daniel
Information Warfare

2008

MANOUVRIER Bernard, LAURENT Ménard
Application Integration: EAI, B2B, BPM and SOA

PAPY Fabrice
Digital Libraries

2006

CORNIOU Jean-Pierre
Looking Back and Going Forward in IT

Lightning Source UK Ltd.
Milton Keynes UK
UKHW021950100719

345918UK00004B/347/P

9 781848 217553